Early Childhood Education and Care in the 21st Century:

Global Guidelines and Papers From an

International Symposium Hosted by

the World Organization for Early Childhood Education

(Organisation Mondiale pour L'Éducation Préscolaire) and

the Association for Childhood Education International

Ruschlikon, Switzerland

July 5-8, 1999

Introduction

The International Symposium on Early Childhood Education and Care for the 21st Century, cosponsored by the World Association for Early Childhood Education (Organisation Mondiale pour l'Éducation Préscolaire [OMEP]) and the Association for Childhood Education International (ACEI), was held in Ruschlikon, Switzerland, July 5-8, 1999. One hundred early childhood education professionals from around the world were invited to attend; 83 were able to be present. They gathered as representatives of the global professional community to work on international guidelines for the education and care of young children. The delegates to the Symposium were selected by the OMEP Symposium Commission and the ACEI Symposium Committee. ACEI and OMEP appointed recorders to record the discussions

This unique event was the first time that Early Childhood Education professionals from 28 diverse nations convened to consider their common professional issues and to work together to produce a document. The Symposium represented four days of intense effort on the part of the delegates to investigate the possibilities of global agreement. Working Groups composed of 9 to 12 delegates were assigned one of the document categories.

As the Symposium delegates worked to develop a set of basic international guidelines for programs serving the world's children under the age of formal school attendance, several insights came into view. The delegates, regardless of nationality, were strong advocates for children and their families. Their shared visions for the world's children included the involvement of families and communities in the care and education of children; coordination of resources, including community and governmental resources; recognition of family and cultural diversity; and a strong belief in the equality of services for all children.

The enormous task of arriving at statements of agreement in the Working Groups was accomplished by the delegates, despite national, cultural, language, and personal differences. While the commonalties abounded, the ways of expressing them and the priorities that should be assigned were more problematic.

The documents produced by the Working Groups were extensive. The content of the seven papers that emerged overlapped in many ways. The common concerns of the delegates emerged regardless of which topic the group had been asked to address. For example, all papers stressed the need to recognize family and cultural diversity and to coordinate efforts and services on behalf of children and families. The shortened version of those documents that appears here attempts to limit the overlap and to provide a more concise summary of the excellent work produced by the Working Groups. This shortened version was developed by a team of editors selected from the delegates.

Because of the international focus, and the hope that the material will be useful to all nations, the document is less comprehensive and less specific than many existing documents. For example, many nations currently have extensive, explicit requirements for the establishment of child care centers, including detailed regulations for staff qualifications, space, and equipment. The Symposium document is intended to serve as an overall rubric under which nations can fit their own more specific rules and regulations.

The most important aspect of the Symposium is that representatives from the global professional community worked together to attempt to get agreement on the most basic components. The Symposium did not intend to develop new guidelines to replace suitable, functional guidelines that are already in use in many nations. Instead, the statements should be useful to those nations that are just beginning to establish policies about the settings for the care and education of the young child, and serve as comparative information for all nations. It represents the first set of documents produced by the global early childhood education professional community and it is hoped that the document will be a starting point to help improve conditions for the world's children in the coming century.

This publication includes a list of the Symposium delegates and text of three papers presented at the Symposium, in addition to the guidelines document. The guidelines document (pp. 5-15) may be freely copied as long as it is noted that the content is from the Document of the International Symposium for Early Childhood Education and Care for the 21st Century. Gottleib Duttweiler Institute, Ruschlikon, Switzerland. July 1999. Contact ACEI for further information.

Acknowledgments

Gratitude is expressed to the Gottleib Duttweiler Institute of Ruschlikon, Switzerland, for the use of their facilities and the encouragement offered, which made this Symposium possible. Appreciation is also expressed to the Symposium Chairs, Leah Adams, Ulla Grob-Menges and Sue Wortham, for their leadership, and to the delegates for the effort and time commitment involved.   Many of the delegates were personally responsible for all expenses required for their attendance. Their personal commitment to the world's children through giving of time and resources is commended.

Note:
The first section of the guidelines document, Overall Philosophy, Goals, and Policies, can be utilized as an overview of the total document and reflects the purposes of the Symposium.

Hsiao-Yun Chang, Taiwan;
Vivi Germanos-Koutsounadis,
Australia.

(left to right) Robert Glenn, NEA,
Delegate; Bettye Caldwell,
Keynote Speaker; Sharon Lynn
Kagan, NAEYC, Delegate.

(front row): Sue Wortham,
ACEI Chair; Leah Adams,
OMEP Co-Chair;
Ulla Grob-Menges,
ACEI Co-Chair.
(back row): Blanca
Hermosilla, Keynote
Speaker; Aurora Huete,
Colombia.

Shirley Raines, ACEI President,
addresses the delegates; Feland
Meadows translates.

Peter Moss, Keynote Speaker;
in background, Jim Hoot,
ACEI Past President.

GLOBAL GUIDELINES FOR EARLY CHILDHOOD EDUCATION AND CARE IN THE 21ST CENTURY

OVERALL PHILOSOPHY, GOALS, AND POLICIES

Every child should have the opportunity to grow up in a setting that values children, that provides conditions for a safe and secure environment, and that respects diversity. Because children are both the present and the future of every nation, they have needs, rights, and intrinsic worth that must be recognized and supported.

Children must receive appropriate nurture and education within and outside their families from birth onward if they are to develop optimally. Attention to the health, nutrition, education, and psychosocial development of children during their early years is essential for the future well-being of nations and the global community.

Knowledge about human development is more substantial than at any time in history. The new century offers opportunities to consolidate recent gains and respond to new challenges that lie ahead.

We urge that members of the global community:

- Assess the extent to which it has carried out previously made commitments to support the education and development of young children
- Develop and implement a range of policies to advance the provision of an interrelated and flexible continuum of early childhood services
- Allocate resources from national governments, development agencies, governmental and non-governmental organizations, and private and voluntary groups to provide quality services
- Collaborate reciprocally across nations to advance the interests of young children and families.

The following areas must be considered in providing a comprehensive network of early childhood services that offer learning and care for children in the next century:

- Environment and Physical Space of Settings for Children
- Curriculum Content and Pedagogy
- Early Childhood Educators and Caregivers
- Partnership With Families and Communities
- Services for Young Children with Special Needs
- Accountability, Supervision, and Management of Programs for Children

Within each area, special attention must be directed toward:

- Services with equal attention to all children
- Linkages among programs and services for optimal effectiveness and utilization of resources
- Recognition of the value of those who care for and teach young children, including working conditions and appropriate remuneration
- Intergenerational approaches whenever feasible

- Empowerment of communities, families, and children
- A mechanism for adequate and uninterrupted funding
- Cost analysis, monitoring, and evaluation of program quality.

Vigorous pursuit of a plan of action to meet the needs of the world's children will make an essential contribution to the future of individual human potential, to long-term national development, and to global prosperity.

ENVIRONMENT AND PHYSICAL SPACE

The young child's learning environment must be physically and psychologically safe. Physical safety includes the need to protect the child from health hazards that prohibit the child's ability to learn and develop. The need to address the child's psychological safety implies that the overall environment should instill a sense of belonging and well-being for all children. The physical space should be organized to provide a variety of learning experiences for all children of different races, gender, ethnicity, or special needs. Resources within this environment should reflect the cultural experiences and traditions of the children and families using the setting. Overall, this safe environment should empower the child by providing opportunities for exploration, play, and practicing life skills.

1. A Safe Environment and Physical Setting

The environment and physical space is free from physical hazards, including unsafe equipment, pollution, and violence.

The environment provides basic sanitation, safe and nutritious food, potable water, and adequate ventilation, and promotes good health practices.

The environment provides the child with a sense of well-being, belonging, security, and freedom from fear.

Equipment and the physical structure are regularly maintained and cleaned.

2. A Developmentally Stimulating Environment

There are opportunities for frequent and positive child-child and child-adult interactions.

The environment stimulates children to play, explore, and discover.

There are opportunities for children to engage in active play and movement.

The environment is aesthetically pleasing and attractive to the child. There is a variety of colors, textures, surfaces, visual dimensions, and perspectives.

There is an abundance of materials that promote problem solving, critical thinking, and creativity for children with different talents and abilities.

Outdoor play equipment and space provide a variety of movement possibilities.

The environment contains opportunities for the creation and extension of play, such as constructions, gardening, natural habitats, and walking paths.

There are resources from the child's local environment for the child to use, including readily available natural materials.

The space is effectively organized so that materials for play and artistic expression are readily accessible to the child.

The environment contains materials for children to construct their own play things. And children participate in the creation and organization of an evolving environment.

CURRICULUM CONTENT AND PEDAGOGY

Early childhood curriculum includes experiences, routines, and interactions that occur in each child's day in group settings and in family care. Curriculum is a plan that reflects the educational philosophy and provides guidelines for educators and caregivers and the interactions between adults and children who carry out the plan.

The child is at the heart of the curriculum. All children are competent and their learning must be rooted in experiences appropriate to their developmental levels and cultures. A quality early childhood curriculum is focused on the whole child and considers physical, cognitive, linguistic, creative, and social and emotional growth. The ultimate goal of an early childhood curriculum is to produce more competent, caring, and empathic world citizens.

The link between learning and development called curriculum results in the following benefits for young children:

- A sense of trust
- A personal identity and sense of mastery
- Positive self-concept and resiliency
- Skills in communication and literacy
- Critical thinking to solve problems and make decisions
- Skills, attitudes, and imagination necessary for construction of their own knowledge of different aspects of the world
- Skills in collaboration and social responsibility
- Understanding, appreciation, and acceptance of responsibility for the environment
- Human values and capability in dealing with moral dilemmas and nonviolent solutions to problems
- A sense of identity and pride in their own cultural, linguistic, and social background, as well as respect for diversity.

1. The Curriculum Document
A plan exists for fostering children's learning.

Flexible, comprehensive plans that are oriented to the child, family, and cultural contexts are implemented.

2. Content of the Curriculum
The curriculum in early childhood programs gives children the opportunity to master information and practice the skills that they need in order to function effectively in society.

The early childhood curriculum emphasizes content that is connected to real world experiences, values, hopes, dreams, and expectations of families and communities. Young children are active contributors to the curriculum.

3. Pedagogical Methods
Educators/caregivers must develop a supportive teaching and caring relationship with children.

Educators/caregivers must possess a basic understanding of pedagogical principles that provide guidelines for practice.

Educators/caregivers have an expansive repertoire of methods upon which they can draw to recognize the children's own learning strategies and support the learning of every child.

4. Learning Materials
Educators/caregivers use local and natural materials as resources for teaching and learning.

Adequate curriculum materials and equipment are provided that are appropriate to the children's special needs and that maintain the integrity of their own culture, such as art, music, dance, and drama.

5. Assessment of Children's Progress
Each child's strengths and assets are recognized. Individual progress is monitored and shared with parents and families in appropriate ways.

Young children learn the skills of self-evaluation and their learning is evaluated, not only in terms of knowledge, but also in terms of their learning processes and performance.

6. Evaluation of Programs
The program is evaluated regularly, using criteria that consider the overall contributions and relevance of the program to every child and the society.

The program is comprehensively and continuously evaluated in terms of its attainment of local, regional, national, and international standards for excellence in the care and education of young children.

EARLY CHILDHOOD EDUCATORS AND CAREGIVERS

Educating and caring for young children is one of the most important and demanding responsibilities that an individual can assume. It is crucial that educators and caregivers possess appropriate characteristics for assuming those responsibilities, knowledge, and skills related to the developmental level of the children, and knowledge of effective programming.

1. Knowledge and Performance
The early childhood educator/caregiver:

• Has a knowledge of child growth, development, and learning

- Is able to apply knowledge of child growth, development, and learning into practice
- Has knowledge of the use of space, materials, and time in order to adapt them appropriately to the needs of the children and in relation to the program that is being implemented
- Is able to communicate effectively with children, colleagues, and families
- Has the ability to work collaboratively and in partnerships with others
- Is able to understand and implement an effective program
- Is able to use a variety of learning materials
- Has the ability to reflect on his/her practice and make any appropriate changes.

2. Personal and Professional Characteristics
The early childhood educator/caregiver:

- Exhibits personal characteristics that demonstrate caring, acceptance, sensitivity, empathy, and warmth toward others
- Has the ability to work collaboratively and in partnership with others
- Exhibits a personal commitment to lifelong learning
- Is an advocate for children and their families.

3. Moral/Ethical Dimensions
The early childhood educator/caregiver:

- Respects the child
- Respects the child's culture and the family practices
- Shows courage to act on behalf of the child and to speak up for the protection of the child
- Is able to frame moral/ethical responses that transcend the immediate issue.

PARTNERSHIP WITH FAMILIES AND COMMUNITIES

The care and education of the child is a shared responsibility among the family, educators and caregivers, and the community. Within the family and community, all participants share an ethical/moral responsibility to promote the optimum conditions for the well-being of children.
The program policies should:

- Promote partnership and positive constructive relationship with families and community
- Provide opportunities for families to participate at different levels, based on their strengths and life experiences
- Support the development of positive, constructive relationships between educators/caregivers and children, between children, and between educators/caregivers and families
- Provide support for families, either directly or through links with other community resources.

1. Communication With Families
Information about the philosophy, policies, procedures is shared in a variety of ways.

There are ongoing discussions and conferences between educator/caregiver and family concerning the child's progress and other issues of concern to family in a language understood by parents.

When feasible, opportunities are provided for children to become familiar with the setting and for educators and caregivers to become acquainted with the families prior to a child's participation in the program.

An informal/formal review is conducted summarizing events of the year.

Resources are available for families to support child development and learning.

2. Moral/Ethical Responsibilities and Behaviors

There are procedures for protection of the child.

There are procedures to protect the confidentiality of information about the family.

Experiences foster self-esteem and self-confidence in all the participants in the setting.

Moral/spiritual/ethical experiences in the curriculum reflect and promote values of individual families.

3. Training/Education Policies

Guidelines are established for parent participation and involvement in the setting.

Information is made available to parents on aspects of child development and learning.

Materials and/or information sessions are made available to parents that are suitable for the culture and geographical location.

Materials for parents are developed for the community and adapted to the sociocultural and geographical location.

4. Recognition of Diversity

The setting exhibits respect, tolerance, and acceptance of all forms of diversity, including culture, ethnicity, age, language, religion, gender, social economic status, family composition, and special needs.

Opportunities are provided for ongoing training of educators and caregivers to enhance knowledge and understanding about issues of diversity.

Materials and strategies ensure participation and engagement of families with diverse characteristics.

5. Transition of Children From Home to the Setting

Information on the expectations of the setting and the curriculum is disseminated to families.

Opportunities are provided for children to become familiar with the setting and educators and caregivers to become acquainted with the families, prior to the beginning of the program when feasible.

Connections between home and the setting are encouraged and maintained.

6. Opportunities for Family and Community Participation
Opportunities are provided for families and community representatives to observe program activities.

Activities and materials are provided to help families support learning at home.

Collaboration is established with families for monitoring children's progress and assessment.

Collaboration is established with families and community representatives for program planning, management, and evaluation.

Families and community representatives participate as advisers and/or decision makers.

Opportunities are provided for volunteering, such as assisting in the classroom and contributing parental expertise skills to the setting when feasible, or enabling families to construct educational materials for use with the children.

7. Interprofessional Collaboration
Collaboration is established with psychologists, social workers, health visitors, businesses, public services, schools, religious groups, leisure services, and family associations.

Support is provided for families in need.

YOUNG CHILDREN WITH SPECIAL NEEDS

Children with special needs are those with impairments, disabilities, illnesses, risks associated with developmental delay, or exceptional abilities/talents. In order to develop to their potential, these children require support services beyond those that are considered sufficient for the development of their same-age peers. The special needs may be due to a wide variety of factors, including:

- Genetic factors (e.g., recognized syndromes)
- Biological/health-related factors (e.g., poor nutrition, prenatal drug exposure, low birth weight, vision/hearing problems)
- Neurological factors (e.g., learning disabilities)
- Psychosocial factors (e.g., mental and behavioral disorders)
- Sociocultural conditions (e.g., bias based on race, ethnicity, language, immigration/refugee status)
- Particular environmental conditions (e.g., abuse, neglect, extreme poverty, trauma).

Children's special needs may range from those requiring minimal attention to those requiring extensive modifications and/or services. The concept of special needs is socially constructed and, because each society is unique, each will develop a meaningful concept of special needs, identify gaps in services, and develop a plan for attendant services provisions. However, all societies should:

- Concentrate on providing funding and other resources to adequately meet these special needs
- Finance ongoing program development, implementation, and evaluation
- Create and enhance societal acceptance of children with special needs
- Organize preservice and inservice professional training for teachers and other service providers to cater to all levels of special educational needs
- Support families and communities in coping with children's special needs
- Emphasize early identification and intervention.

Goals for nations to work toward in serving children with all needs include:

1. Access and Equity of Services
Both female and male children have equal access and equity in types and levels of support.

Children from low-income groups have access and equity similar to that of high-income groups.

Children from all types of communities (e.g., urban, rural) have similar access and equity.

Children have access and equity irrespective of their religious, ethnic, language, or cultural affiliation.

Policymakers include equal access and equity standards in public policy.

Information about opportunities for access and equity of services are made available to all groups through culturally relevant and effective media channels.

2. Basic Health and Nutrition
Policies and funding for educating mothers and educators/caregivers about proper nutrition and health practices is available to both reduce the incidence of special needs and to provide support.

This includes providing parents and community members with information to enable them to make appropriate decisions about children's health care.

3. Common Philosophy and Common Aims
A multi- or trans-disciplinary team is composed of the parents and staff relevant to meeting the particular child's needs.

There is an identified person for planning, coordinating, and monitoring the delivery of services.

Policymakers request written, individual plans for all children.
Policymakers require review and revision of such plans on a regular basis.

4. Staff and Service Providers

At least one staff member and/or service provider in a setting has the skills to identify the special needs of children.

Staff members and/or service providers are able to individualize and make appropriate modifications for education and care.

Staff members and/or service providers are able to establish ongoing relationships with parents/guardians and families in meeting the needs of their children.

Staff members and/or service providers should be skilled in dealing with policymakers, as well as community agencies, when collaborating to meet children's needs.

5. Adaptations to Indoor and Outdoor Environments

The ratio of adults to children allows individual needs of all children to be met.

Adaptive equipment and materials to facilitate special needs children's full involvement in the environment is provided.

6. Services Delivery

Services are delivered to the greatest extent possible within an inclusive environment of special needs children and non-special needs children.

Families are involved in decision making, planning, delivery, and assessment of services.

To the maximum extent possible, the child with special needs is actively included in the life of the community.

7. Responsiveness to Individual Needs

Staff and service providers demonstrate awareness, knowledge, and understanding of the developmental, cultural, religious, and gender variables associated with the special needs children they serve.

Staff and service providers facilitate acceptance and inclusion of all children, regardless of differences in developmental level, culture, religion, or gender.

Advocacy for programs and services for all children with special needs is pursued.

ACCOUNTABILITY, SUPERVISION, AND MANAGEMENT

Young children and their families have a right to equitable access to services. Children are entitled to quality early education services; therefore, accountability mechanisms need to be community-based, open and transparent, respectful of diversities and multiple perspectives, and should foster active participation of family and community.

Approaches to supervision and management address the following:

- Enhancing the relationship between educator/caregiver and children
- Providing a professional climate that encourages competence and sound pedagogical practices
- Enhancing the sense of shared partnership between early education and care programs with families and communities, and fostering, to the greatest degree feasible, local and regional decision making regarding early care and education policies
- Ensuring high-quality services to children and families
- Ensuring the well-being of all children as a shared responsibility of the government, community, professional organizations, families, and educators/caregivers.

1. Policies for Quality Standards

Governmental expenditures for children under school age are adequate to provide quality services and the supervision and monitoring of programs.

There are clear, identifiable legislative and executive structures (e.g., government ministries and parliaments) and collaboration among and across different levels of government for establishing policy; and the jurisdiction for implementing quality services for young children and families.

There are concrete mechanisms for solicitation of input from the community, families, and professionals responsible for the education and care of children.

There is informed decision making and policy development based on quality research concerning implementation of early education and care services.

Processes are established for community-based dialogue about how the needs of children are addressed to ensure quality program services.

Mechanisms are established for community-wide assessment and evaluation of programs and services.

Processes are established for determining community expectations and guidelines for quality programs and services.

2. Service Delivery

Quality standards are stated, published, and disseminated to policymakers, and professionals in related fields and provide the basis for governmental policy guidelines.

Standards for quality are derived from research, successful past professional practice, and the goals for ensuring the future education and well-being of young children and their families.

Adequate professional training and qualification systems are in place to ensure that those who work with young children and their families have the

knowledge and skills to optimally carry out their responsibilities.
Resources are available to support families in meeting the needs of their
young children (e.g., health services, information services about programs,
public spaces for play, libraries).

Resources are available to support program services and educators/
caregivers in meeting the needs of children (e.g., pre- and inservice training,
program improvement, capital improvement).

Mechanisms are established to ensure that community resources are shared
among programs and that coordination of available resources takes place.

3. **Professional Associations for Educators and Caregivers and Policymakers**
Results of research studies are widely accessible through conferences, internal
distribution, clearinghouses, and other professional development programs.

High-quality educational materials are developed, reviewed, evaluated, and
made available to members and constituencies of professional organizations
and governmental information dissemination centers.

Professional associations make available information and contacts for individuals and groups to secure funding for appropriate projects and activities,
and to be effective advocates on behalf of children and families.

Professional organizations are represented on significant government commit-
tees and are in the position to influence decisions regarding governmental
policies and programs.

Recommendations and position papers of professional organizations are
incorporated into the laws, regulations, and accountability systems of early
education and care programs.

Effective alliances are formed among professional organizations to establish
and reach the goals of providing education and care to the world's children.

4. **Program and Educator Responsibilities**
Educators/caregivers are responsible for planning and implementing high-
quality early education and care programs in partnership with parents and
community and in compliance with governmental policy guidelines and
professional standards disseminated by professional organizations.

Information and referral procedures to other community programs and
services are established.

Procedures to support children's transition to formal schooling are established.

Educators/caregivers are encouraged to meet higher program standards for
accreditation or special recognition, such as influencing changes in guidelines, laws, or regulations.

Symposium Delegates

Leah Adams (U.S.A.)
Christie A. Ade-Ajayi (Nigeria)
Lieselotte Ahnert (U.S.A.)
Jacqueline Andries (Belgium)
Eric Atmore (South Africa)
Ann C. Barbour (U.S.A.)
Dianne Bascombe (Canada)
Sandra Beckman (Canada)
Doris Bergen (U.S.A.)
Jacqueline Blackwell (U.S.A.)
Jeffrey Brewster (Belgium)
Bettye M. Caldwell (U.S.A.)
Anarella Cellitti (Venezuela)
Hsiao-Yun Chang (Taiwan)
Chu-Ying Chien (Taiwan)
Hui-Ling Chua (Singapore)
Rhonda Clements (U.S.A.)
Sandra Crosser (U.S.A.)
Audrey Curtis (England)
Blanche Desjean-Perrotta (U.S.A.)
Josephine M. Desouza (U.S.A.)
Frederick N. Ebbeck (Australia)
Marjory Ebbeck (Australia)
E. Anne Eddowes (U.S.A.)
Eila Estola (Finland)
W. E. Fthenakis (Germany)
Vivi Germanos-Koutsounadis (Australia)
Mark R. Ginsberg (U.S.A.)
Robert Glenn (U.S.A.)
Eugenia Gonzalez M. (Spain)
Rolf Grafwallner (U.S.A.)
Ulla Grob-Menges (Switzerland)
Hans-Ulrich Grunder (Switzerland)
Blanca Hermosilla M. (Chile)
Joan E. Herwig (U.S.A.)
James L. Hoot (U.S.A.)
Aurora Huete (Colombia)
Eeva Hujala (Finland)
Rosa Iglesias (Spain)
Mary Renck Jalongo (U.S.A.)

Lynne Jasik (Israel)
Priti Joshi (U.S.A.)
Sharon Lynn Kagan (U.S.A.)
Venita Kaul (India)
Linda LeBlanc (U.S.A.)
Maria Paz Lebrero (Spain)
Sandra Lesibu (U.S.A.)
Martha Llanos (Peru)
Deborah Eville Lo (U.S.A.)
Ebele J. Maduewesi (Nigeria)
Mahenaz Mahmud (Pakistan)
Tata J. Mbugua (Kenya)
Anna P. McArthur (U.S.A.)
Feland L. Meadows (U.S.A.)
Samira M. Moosa (U.S.A.)
Mari Mori (Japan)
Peter Moss (England)
Barbara Kimes Myers (U.S.A.)
Margaret A. Nicholls (New Zealand)
Heinrich Nufer (Switzerland)
Patricia P. Olmsted (U.S.A.)
Jyotsna Pattnaik (U.S.A.)
Victoria Peralta M. (Chile)
Candide Pineault (Canada)
Lucio Pusci (Italy)
James Quisenberry (U.S.A.)
Nancy L. Quisenberry (U.S.A.)
Shirley Raines (U.S.A.)
Nirmala Rao (Hong Kong)
Wilma Robles de Meléndez (U.S.A.)
Jillian Rodd (England)
Beatriz Saal (Argentina)
Ingrid Pramling Samuelson (Sweden)
Elizabeth Sestini (England)
Irene Sever (Israel)
Mary Sue Singletary (U.S.A.)
Lynn Staley (U.S.A.)
Leena Tauriainen (Finland)
Lenore Wineberg (U.S.A.)
Sue C. Wortham (U.S.A.)

SYMPOSIUM CHAIRS

Leah Adams, OMEP Co-Chair
Ulla Grob-Menges, OMEP Co-Chair
Sue C. Wortham, ACEI Chair

GUIDELINES DOCUMENT EDITORS
Leah Adams
Audrey Curtis
Mary Renck Jalongo
Sue C. Wortham

WORKING GROUP DOCUMENT EDITORS
Ann C. Barbour
Doris Bergen
Hui-Ling Chua
Rolf Grafwallner
Lucio Pusci
Nancy L. Quisenberry
Elizabeth Sestini

LANGUAGE DOCUMENT EDITORS
Hsiao-Yun Chang
Chu-Ying Chien
Victoria Peralta

ACEI SYMPOSIUM PLANNING COMMITTEE
Sue C. Wortham, Chair
James L. Hoot
Jacqueline Blackwell
Nancy L. Quisenberry
Maria Olivia Herrera
Jillian Rodd
Betty Sun Chao

Committee Resources
Nancy Brown (ACEI United Nations
  Representative)
Hans-Ulrich Grunder
Mary Renck Jalongo

OMEP SYMPOSIUM PLANNING COMMISSION
Leah Adams, Chair
Ulla Grob-Menges, Co-Chair and
  Executive Liaison
Lynne Jasik
Venita Kaul
Mapitso Malepa
Miyako Ohto
Haydee Davila Olvera
Candide Peneault
Ingrid Pramling Samuelson

International Standards or One of Many Possibilities?*

Peter Moss
Peter Moss is Professor of Early Childhood Provision, Thomas Coram Research Unit, Institute of Education, University of London.

The two main points I want to make may seem at odds with the main goal of the Symposium—but I am assured that you welcome alternative perspectives. First, I want to point out the problematic nature of developing a set of international guidelines or standards for programmes serving children under the age of 6. I will argue that this goal arises from the adoption of a particular philosophical perspective; viewed from other perspectives, it may not be feasible or desirable. Second, I want to question how we can prepare ourselves to undertake early childhood work in the 21st century, given that we can have no idea of the political, social, cultural, economic, or environmental conditions that will develop. Could a group meeting in 1899 have predicted the conditions of 1919, 1939, or 1999?

"Quality Targets in Services for Young Children"
Before explaining why I find the idea of international guidelines problematic, let me tell you something about my experience in this field. Between 1986 and 1996, I co-ordinated the European Commission Network on Childcare and Other Measures To Reconcile Employment and Family Responsibilities (EC Childcare Network for short)—a group funded by the European Commission and consisting of an expert from each member state. We had three main interests: men as caretakers, both as fathers and workers in children's services; parental leave and other forms of leave to help parents reconcile employment and caring for children; and services providing care, education, and recreation for children from 0 to 10 (for a full account of the network and its work, see EC Childcare Network, 1996).

Within our work, the subject of quality became a priority. We began with a European seminar held in Barcelona in 1991, which led to a very important discussion paper: *Quality in Services for Young Children* (Balaguer, Mestres, & Penn, 1991). It culminated in the 1995 publication of a report titled *Quality Targets in Services for Young Children.* Both documents were translated into all official EU languages and were very widely disseminated.

Both the discussion paper and *Quality Targets* were drafted by Irene Balaguer from Spain and Helen Penn from Britain, and discussed by Network members from all the EU member states. I want to emphasise that our work in this field was the product of a unique process of European dialogue and collaboration that took place over many years. There is nothing else like it, at least in the field of early childhood. It is an illustration of what can be done by working together cross-nationally, seeking common ground while recognising and valuing difference.

**Editor's Note: We have retained the British spelling in this paper.*

Let me return to the history of the *Quality Targets* document. In 1992, the
EU Council of Ministers—that is, all member states—adopted a Council Recommendation on Child Care (92/241/EEC). Unlike a Directive, a Council Recommendation is not a legally binding measure. It is, however, an expression of
political commitment and an important statement of common principles and
objectives. The Recommendation calls for measures that would enable parents
to reconcile employment with the care and upbringing of children. Measures
should be taken in four areas: men taking more responsibility for children's
care, making the workplace more responsive to parents, parental leave, and
what the document calls "child care services." (I should note that the Network
found the EU concept of "child care services," and the implied focus on children
with employed parents, very problematic, and we always emphasised the need
for services for *all* children and families.)

In the case of these "child care services," the Recommendation proposed a
number of specific objectives for the development of services for young children:

- Affordability
- Access to services in all areas, both urban and rural
- Access to services for children with special needs
- Safety and security within a pedagogical approach
- Close and responsive relations among services, parents, and local
  communities
- Diversity and flexibility of services
- Increased choice for parents
- Coherence among services.

Taken together, these objectives form the basis for one definition of a good
quality service system. However, such objectives are not likely to emerge of their
own accord. The Network argued that specific conditions are needed to enable
the achievement of these objectives, including:

- A policy framework for service provision
- Co-ordination of responsibility for services
- A curricular framework
- Appropriate staffing and staff conditions (including training and pay)
- Appropriate physical environments
- Infrastructure for planning, monitoring, support, training, research, and
  development
- Adequate financing of services and infrastructure.

What the Network tried to do in *Quality Targets* is set out a number of pro-
posals for making progress towards achieving both the objectives and the conditions. Therefore, *Quality Targets* needs to be considered within the political
framework provided by the Council Recommendation on Child Care, a policy
document to which all governments have agreed. *Quality Targets* should be
considered one attempt to give meaning and direction to the broad principles
and objectives contained in that political document.

What are these quality targets? The report proposes 40 targets: some apply
to national or regional levels of government, some to local levels of government
(communes), and some to individual centres. The 40 targets are divided into 8
blocks:

- Policy
- Finance
- Levels and Types of Services
- Education
- Staff-Child Ratios
- Staff Employment and Training
- Environment and Health
- Parents and Community
- Performance.

Each block starts with a discussion section, followed by a number of targets. Each block ends with examples, drawn from all over Europe. These examples show how particular targets already have been achieved in different countries.

I do not propose to go through the targets now. I will, however, outline a few by way of illustration. Target 1 seeks "a coherent statement of intent for care and education services to young children 0-6," and Target 2 refers to the need for one department—at national, regional, and local levels—to take responsibility for implementing the policy. The first two targets, therefore, express a view that services for young children—from 0 to 6—need to be integrated and coherent, and developed within a single national policy framework.

Target 7 addresses funding: "Public expenditure on services for young children (in this case defined as children aged 5 years and under) should be not less than 1% of GDP in order to meet targets set for services, both for children under three and over three." We arrived at this 1 percent figure as representing about a fifth of what EU member states currently spend on all forms of education. We concluded that, in this context, 1 percent of GDP was a reasonable share of resources for young children.

Target 11 addresses levels of provision. Publicly funded services should offer full-time equivalent places for: at least 90 percent of children aged 3-6 years, and at least 15 percent of children under 3. This is an example of the Network's efforts to find targets that would be feasible for all countries to achieve over 10 years. We recognised that a 15 percent provision for children under 3 is probably well below what is needed, but it would be a significant improvement for many countries that currently have provision for less than 5 percent. Once again, I emphasise that the targets are provisional and the document makes clear that countries or regions that already have achieved some or all of the targets can and should go on to set new ones.

Target 16 states that "all collective services for young children 0-6 whether in the public or private sector should have coherent values and objectives including a stated and explicit educational philosophy." Here, the Network wanted to emphasise the importance of education in all services, whether for children under or over 3, and to recognise children as active learners from birth. At the same time, the document avoids being too prescriptive about the nature of the educational philosophy and the content of education, recognising the importance of diversity (this is discussed in Target 18).

Finally, I want to mention two targets on staff employment and training. Target 26 deals with staff training:

A minimum of 60% of staff working directly with children in collective services should have a grant eligible basic training of at least three years at a post-18 level, which incorporates both the theory and practice of pedagogy and child development. All training should be modular. All staff in services (both collective and family day care) who are not trained to this level should have right of access to such training including on an inservice basis.

Target 29 proposes that "20% of staff employed in collective services should be men." Unfortunately, this was the one target where we were not able to find any examples of achievement at a national level—in every country, more than 95 percent of staff in services for young children are women.

I want to conclude my comments about *Quality Targets* by mentioning the concept of quality that informed this document and the other work of the EC Childcare Network. From the start, it was clear to Network members that a single, universal, objective concept of quality was impossible—not least because any definition of quality is values based and context specific. Indeed, this is the first of a series of assumptions that we spell out as underlying the Network's approach to quality:

- Quality is a relative concept, based on values and beliefs
- Defining quality is a process and this process is important in its own right, providing opportunities to share, discuss, and understand values, ideas, knowledge, and experience
- The process should be participatory and democratic, involving children, parents and families, and professionals working in services
- The needs, perspectives, and values of these groups may sometimes differ
- Defining quality should be seen as a dynamic and continuous process, involving regular review and never reaching a final, "objective" statement.

The Network developed the *Quality Targets in Services for Young Children* within a very specific political and ethical framework: The Council Recommendation on Child Care. Another framework would have produced other targets. *Quality Targets* was the product of a long-term process, involving much discussion and extensive consultation. We tried to avoid being too prescriptive in areas such as educational philosophy and practice. We sought to leave room for interpretation in most of the targets, recognising the diversity of tradition and context in Europe: "The targets do not require standardisation of service systems, philosophies or working methods, but support for common objectives and principles." We did not offer the *Quality Targets* as the one and only standard, nor as the final word; indeed, as we say at the end, "reaching these targets would not be the end of the search for quality; that is a dynamic and continuous process, involving regular reflection and review."

The Problem With "International Guidelines" or "International Standards"
This introduction, I hope, shows that I come to this discussion of guidelines and standards with some experience. My problem with concepts such as "international guidelines" or "international standards" is not just based on abstract theories, but rather is grounded in an ambitious attempt to develop European guidelines on quality. In the end, the Childcare Network rejected a search for *the* European guidelines. We settled instead for offering *one* of many possible perspectives. At the time, the Network was already identifying some of the problems with the search for universal guidelines and even with the use of the term "guidelines," which easily can be viewed as normative and normalising.

Since then, I have been working to deepen my understanding of why I find the concept of "international guidelines" or "standards" to be problematic—as well as concepts such as "quality," "excellence," and "best practice." This work has produced two books: an edited volume, *Valuing Quality in Early Childhood Services* (Moss & Pence, 1994), and *Beyond Quality in Early Childhood Education and Care: Postmodern Perspectives*, written with Alan Pence and Gunilla Dahlberg (Dahlberg, Moss, & Pence, 1999). I also gained a lot of inspiration and insight from work in Reggio Emilia, to which I shall return.

I want to suggest five related reasons for finding the idea of international guidelines to be problematic: the ethical and political dimension, the importance of context, the value of dissensus and difference, power and its effects, and the philosophical perspective from which we understand our world. I do not have time to develop any in detail. All I can do is raise them and refer you to *Beyond Quality* for further discussion.

The first reason is ethical and political. I want to argue that:

- There is no such thing as "the child" or "childhood," an essential being and state waiting to be discovered, defined, and realised; rather, there are many children and many childhoods, each constructed by our "understandings of childhood and what children are and should be"
- That the purposes and projects of early childhood institutions are not self-evident, but can be many and varied
- That we can understand learning and knowledge in many ways
- That we cannot discuss early childhood institutions without discussing what might be called broader "good life" questions, such as what do we want for our children, both here and now and in the future, and what is a good childhood.

The answers to these issues—who is the child, what is the early childhood institution, what is knowledge and learning, what is the good life—cannot be revealed through application of the supposedly objective, scientific method. They are all essentially philosophical and moral, value-laden and political. As Readings (1996) comments, "they raise questions that are philosophical in that they are fundamentally incapable of producing cognitive certainty or definitive answers. . . . [and] will necessarily give rise to further debate for they are radically at odds with the logic of quantification." They involve us making choices—choices for which we must then take responsibility. It follows that pedagogical work with young children is necessarily a political and ethical project.

This is the position taken by the early childhood educators in Reggio Emilia. They say that their experience is only one of many possibilities; that they made their choice from among these many possibilities; that behind every solution and organisation is a choice of values and ethics—a social and political choice; and that their work is not a recipe or model that can be copied, because values can only be lived not copied. One of their most important choices has been to understand the child as rich, competent, and intelligent—a co-constructor of knowledge, a researcher actively seeking to make meaning of the world. In doing so, they have decided against choosing other understandings or constructions of the child, which have been very productive in other types of pedagogy and other areas of work with children: for example, the child as knowledge reproducer, or as an innocent, or the child as nature, "an essential being of universal properties and inherent capabilities whose development is innate, biologically determined and follows general laws." Reggio also has rejected the construction of the "child at risk" or "in need," not only because the construction produces a "poor child," but also because they have chosen, in the words of Carlina Rinaldi (former director of early childhood services in Reggio), "to move from the child as a subject of needs to a subject of rights."

It is important to add that Reggio educators understand that values are involved in not only how they choose to understand the child, but also how they choose to organise and structure their early childhood services, for example in their staffing arrangements and their organisation of staff time. In short, even the most functional guideline or target has a moral and political dimension.

Let me give you another example of this issue of choices to be made, choices that are inescapably moral and political. In *Beyond Quality in Early Childhood Education and Care*, we argue that

from a social constructionist perspective [early childhood institutions], as well as our images of what a child is, can be and should be, must be seen as the social construction of a community of human agents, originating through our active interaction with other people and with society. . . . [Early childhood] institutions and pedagogical practises for children are constituted by dominant discourses in our society and embody thoughts, conceptions and ethics which prevail at a given moment in a given society. (p. 62)

An increasingly dominant construction of the early childhood institution, at least in the Anglo-American world, portrays it as a processing plant of children producing outcomes that are standardised and predetermined by adults: the metaphor, as Lilian Katz (1993) points out, is the factory. Influenced by Reggio, in our new book we suggest another construction of these institutions: as *public forums in civil society in which adults and children participate together in projects of social, cultural, political, and economic significance.* The range of projects is many and varied, and we discuss just some of the possibilities. If we choose to view them in this way, early childhood institutions are places of childhood and part of life, rather than places for realising adult performance and preparing for life.

The example of Reggio contributes to the second reason why I am uneasy with aspirations to universality. The Reggio experience developed within a very particular political, economic, and social context, and draws on a very particular historical experience. Therefore, again, Reggio is not a model to be copied. In psychology, universal assumptions increasingly are regarded as problematic, leading to a recognition of the profound significance of context, giving precedence to contingency over universality. Rogoff and Chavajay (1995), in discussing recent developments in cultural cognition, conclude that "inherent to socio-cultural approaches is a premise that individual, social and cultural levels are inseparable." In his recent book on cultural psychology, Michael Cole (1996) questions the way that context often is treated as additional or peripheral. Instead, he conceptualises context as "that which weaves together," precluding the possibility of separating context out as an independent variable—treating it instead as profound, transformative, and inextricably interwoven.

The question raised by these debates is whether and how international guidelines can address this singularity, the product of the specificities of temporal and spatial context. Indeed, we can ask the more fundamental question: Why should we want to offer universal order rather than the singularity of local experience? And what might the consequences be of trying to do so?

This point leads to my third reason. The striving for international guidelines carries within it, I think, the values of consensus, sameness, and foreclosure—to get to the end, to find common ground, to reach a final agreement. I would want to argue instead for the values of dissensus, difference, and "keeping the question of meaning open as a locus for debate." Several issues are key here. First, we are called to deepen understanding and enrich practice; indeed, we are stimulated to think through the dynamic of diversity and confrontation, using that term in its Italian sense of exchanging and debating different perspectives. At a lecture, I heard Gilles Deleuze put it this way: "Thought and concepts can be seen as a consequence of the provocation of an encounter. Thought is what confronts us from the outside unexpectedly. Something in the world forces us to think." He also says that we can begin to "explore the paradoxical sides of life, and the possible, through offering a multiplicity of ways of existing in the world" and that we should "not interpret events from a totalizing principle [that] robs situations of their singularity."

Second, if we believe in democratic and emancipatory values, then those must find a place in early childhood work. Seyla Benhabib (1992) observes, in relation to moral discussion, that "it is the process of dialogue, conversation and mutual understanding, and not consensus, [that] is our goal." Zygmunt Bauman (1997) puts the matter even more graphically: "Consensus and unanimity augur the tranquillity of the graveyard . . . it is in the graveyard of universal consensus that responsibility and freedom and the individual exhale their last sigh."

I think the issue goes even further, however. It takes us to a major ethical issue: How do we relate to the Other, without assimilating the Other into being the same? How do we establish forms of knowledge and types of relationships that do not simply turn the Other into the same? Robert Young (1990) observes that "the concept of Totality has dominated Western philosophy in its long history of desire for unity and the One. In Western philosophy, when knowledge or theory comprehends the Other, the alterity of the latter vanishes as it becomes part of the same."

This takes me to my fourth concern. The search for universal guidelines, indeed the very aspiration, raises questions about power and power relations. When we talk about globalisation or internationalisation we need to recognise that these processes do not involve equal exchange and influence among different societies, cultures, and groups. Rather, they involve unequal relationships, which produce what Michel Foucault refers to as *dominant discursive regimes,* or *regimes of truth.* Such discursive regimes organise our everyday experience of the world. They influence or govern our ideas, thoughts, and actions in a specific direction. They exercise power over our thought by directing or governing what we see as the "truth" and how we construct the world, and hence our acting and doing; as such, discourse provides the mechanism for rendering reality amenable to certain kinds of actions (Miller & Rose, 1993). By so doing, they also exclude alternative ways of understanding and interpreting the world.

I would argue that, within current power relations, attempts to produce international early childhood guidelines are likely to be governed by the dominant early childhood discourse, which is Anglo-American, and which is the product of the linguistic, cultural, economic, and technological structure of this one part of the world. This discourse, in turn, is strongly governed by one discipline: developmental psychology. As Mimi Bloch (1992) observes: "The terms critical theory, interpretivist or symbolic research or postmodern are rarely heard in (American) seminar rooms, publications or conferences focusing on early childhood education . . . one reason for [this] lack of alternative perspectives [being] the century-long domination of psychological and child development perspectives in the field of early childhood education." The issue is not whether this early childhood discourse is right or wrong—but rather that it offers only one perspective, one type of knowledge, one set of truths, from many possibilities. And that this perspective, knowledge, and truth produces a particular construction of the young child, of early childhood, and of the early childhood institution.

I would add that we can understand the dominant Anglo-American discourse about early childhood—and the policy, practice, and research it produces—in the context of the particular form of capitalism that has become dominant in the Anglo-American world, and is becoming ever more influential in other parts of the world. This form of neo-liberal capitalism emphasises free markets and the commodification of all activities and relationships; competition and the necessity of inequalities; contractual relationships with predetermined and measurable outcomes; individual responsibility and autonomy; the primacy of shareholder value and business values; flexible employment and lifelong learning to fulfil the shifting needs of the labour market; short-term time frames and the desire for solutions, to know "what works." Correct solutions are valued over critical questions. To be correct, solutions must be final, clear-cut, and universal. Hence, our obsession with programmes, best practice, quality, and planning.

I introduce capitalism here not as a rhetorical device, but rather as a description of the dominant form of economic relations throughout much of the world; and to remind you that capitalism is neither static nor unitary. It is dynamic and takes different forms—and the form it takes constitutes an important part of the context within which early childhood work is organised and practised. The early childhood services in Reggio can be understood in relation to a particular form of capitalist organisation that is widespread in the part of Italy where Reggio is situated, which is characterised by the clustering of small- and medium-size companies producing similar products while managing to combine competition with a capacity to collaborate in matters of mutual interest. So, too, the early childhood services in the U.S. and Britain can be understood in relation to the type of neo-liberal capitalism I have just outlined.

My final reason for questioning the concept of "international guidelines and standards" is that the aspiration to produce such material needs to be self-aware and self-critical, but often is not. Self-awareness should concern not only values, context, difference, and power, but also the broader issue of adopting a particular philosophical position, a particular way of understanding the world. In short, recognition that a philosophical choice has been made, rather than that a self-evident direction has been taken. For, I would argue, "international guidelines" implies a choice to adopt a philosophical framework, a way of understanding the world, which Habermas (1983) refers to as the Project of Modernity. This philosophical perspective has had a powerful hold on the Minority World for more than 300 years. It values certainty, linear progress, order, objectivity, and universality. It believes in a knowable world out there waiting to be revealed and capable of accurate representation.

If, however, you choose to work with complexity, values, diversity, subjectivity, and multiple perspectives, *if* you recognise the temporal and spatial context of institutions, *if* you consider pedagogical work to be political and moral, then you need to consider an alternative choice, which involves a different way of understanding the world—what might be called a postmodern perspective or a "postmodern sensibility" (Popkewitz, 1998). Postmodernity recognises and welcomes uncertainty, complexity, diversity, non-linearity, subjectivity, multiple perspectives, and temporal and spatial specificities. From the perspective of postmodernity, there is no absolute reality waiting "out there" to be discovered, no external position of certainty, no universal understanding that exists outside history and society that can provide foundations for truth, knowledge, and ethics. Instead, the world and our knowledge of it are seen as socially constructed and all of us, children and adults, are active participants in the process.

I have no time to go into this comparison further, as we do in our new book. I would, however emphasise that the Anglo-American discourse in early childhood is permeated by the values and assumptions of modernity. Developmental psychology can be considered, too, in the words of Erica Burman (1994), "a paradigmatically modern discipline arising at a time of commitment to narratives of truth, objectivity, science and reason." Just as concepts like quality, which are very prominent in the Anglo-American modernist discourse, are being problematised, so too is developmental psychology, both from within and without the discipline. If both quality and developmental psychology are, to some degree, in crisis today, it is because both are based on a positivistic programme of "establishing permanent criteria and uncovering an indisputable foundation for knowledge [that has] proved to be unattainable."

In our new book, *Beyond Quality*, Gunilla Dahlberg, Alan Pence, and I argue that Reggio's pedagogical practice is located in a profound understanding of young children in relation to the world and a philosophical perspective that, in many respects, seems to us postmodern—although we recognise that the educators of Reggio do not choose to use such labels. Some of the elements of that practice, understanding, and perspective that lead us to this conclusion include: choosing to adopt a social constructionist approach; challenging and deconstructing dominant discourses, realising the power of these discourses in shaping and governing our thoughts and actions, including the field of early childhood pedagogy; rejecting the prescription of rules, goals, methods, and standards, and in so doing risking uncertainty and complexity; having the courage to think for themselves in constructing new discourses, and in so doing daring to make the choice of understanding the child as a rich child, a child of infinite capabilities, a child born with a hundred languages; building a new pedagogical project, emphasising relationships and encounters, dialogue and negotiation, reflection and critical thinking; crossing the borders of disciplines and perspectives, replacing either/or positions with an and/also openness; and understanding the contextualised and dynamic nature of pedagogical practice, which problematises the idea of a transferable "programme" or a universal project.

Modernity and Postmodernity

Discussion of modernity and postmodernity leads me to my last point. Some would argue that postmodernity and a host of other "posts" add up to us living in a period of fundamental or epochal change. As Kumar (1995) observes, "We are faced at the end of the 20th century with a series of pronouncements and declarations that, taken either singly or together, amount to the claim that the western world is undergoing one of the most profound transformations of its existence." Or, as Patti Lather (1991) says, "We are at a fundamental turning point in social thought, an epochal shift marked by thinking differently about how we think. . . . We seem to be somewhere in the midst of a shift away from the concept of a found world, 'out there,' objective, knowable, factual towards a concept of constructed worlds." Others, however, would question whether we are living through such a fundamental and epochal transition. They would argue that we are experiencing variations of existing conditions and not fundamentally new conditions—indeed, that we are living in conditions of late modernity rather than postmodernity.

However, it seems clear that we are living in times of accelerating and widespread change and this is unlikely to stop or slow down. In these circumstances, I think it is not very useful to speculate about early childhood in the 21st century. Rather, I think we need to develop our abilities to analyse and make sense of the world we live in here and now, and its relationship to early childhood, early childhood institutions, and pedagogical work. One requirement is to cross borders, to broaden our knowledge and understanding of fields beyond psychology and education—fields such as philosophy, ethics, political science, sociology, anthropology, economics, the physical sciences, the environment, and culture in its many forms. This means not only reading more widely ourselves, but also engaging with people from these different disciplines. It also means recognising and insisting upon the relationship between early childhood and the big issues—social, political, cultural, and economic—that confront societies throughout the world: the welfare state, democracy, civil society, capitalism, and the labour market. And it means insisting upon this relationship not just because of the adults young children will become, but also because young children are themselves citizens and early childhood is an important part of life in its own right—not just a state of incomplete adulthood.

Conclusion

I want to conclude by trying to restate my position. I am uneasy with the idea of "international guidelines or standards," for their denial of diversity and their potential for normalisation and control. I have indulged in such an exercise myself, at a European level, a process that increasingly problematised the concept. What we as a European Network self-consciously ended up with was, in the words of Reggio, one choice from among many possibilities. By saying that, I do not devalue the work; indeed, the EC Childcare Network's reports gained credibility and influence by the modesty of their claims and their reluctance to be prescriptive. So, too, this Symposium can work on developing a document, which I am sure will be of great interest and value.

It seems to me, however, that it is important to discuss what claims are made for and by this document. To me, the claim of "international guidelines or standards" are problematic. The claim of offering the perspective of a group self-aware of its own singularity—in terms of the disciplines it uses, of the other influences that shape its understandings, and of the philosophical position it takes—would be a welcome recognition of the values of plurality, dialogue, and "keeping the question of meaning open as a locus for debate."

Let me conclude with a quotation from *Cosmopolis*, Stephen Toulmin's history of modernity (1990), which for me rings many bells about the risks and possibilities that face us:

There may be no rational way to convert to our point of view people who honestly hold other positions, but we cannot short-circuit such disagreements. Instead we should live with them as further evidence of the diversity of human life. . . . Tolerating the resulting plurality, ambiguity, or the lack of certainty is no error. Honest reflection shows it is part of the price we inevitably pay for being human beings and not gods. . . . (pp. 29-30)

Idiosyncrasies of persons and cultures cannot be eliminated. . . . Within a humanized Modernity, the decontextualization of problems so typical of High Modernity is no longer a serious option. . . . [The commentator Walter Lippman once said] "To every human problem there is a solution that is simple, neat and wrong"; and that is as true of intellectual as it is of practical problems. (p. 201)

References

Balaguer, I., Mestres, J., & Penn, H. (1991). *Quality in services for young children.* Brussels: European Commission Equal Opportunities Unit.

Bauman, Z. (1997). *Postmodernity and its discontents.* Cambridge: Polity Press

Benhabib, S. (1992). *Situating the self: Gender, community and postmodernism in contemporary ethics.* Cambridge: Polity Press.

Bloch, M. (1992). Critical perspectives on the historical relationship between child development and early childhood education research. In S. Kessler & B. Swadener (Eds.), *Reconceptualizing the early childhood curriculum.* New York: Teachers College Press.

Burman, E. (1994). *Deconstructing developmental psychology.* London: Routledge.

Cole, M. (1996). *Cultural psychology: A once and future discipline.* Cambridge, MA: Belknap Press.

Dahlberg, G., Moss, P., & Pence, A. (1999). *Beyond quality in early childhood education and care: Postmodern perspectives.* London: Falmer Press.

European Commission Childcare Network. (1995). *Quality targets in services for young children.* Brussels: European Commission Equal Opportunities Unit.

European Commission Childcare Network. (1996). *A decade of achievement.* Brussels: European Commission Equal Opportunities Unit.

Habermas, J. (1983). Modernity: An incomplete project. In H. Foster (Ed.), *The anti-aesthetic; Essays on postmodern culture.* Port Townsend: Washington.

Katz, L. (1993). What can we learn from Reggio-Emilia? In C. Edwards, L. Gandini, & G. Forman (Eds.), *The hundred languages of children* (pp. 19-40). Norwood, NJ: Ablex.

Kumar, K. (1995). *From post-industrial to post-modern society: New theories of the contemporary world.* Oxford: Blackwell.

Lather, P. (1991). *Getting smart: Feminist research and pedagogy with/in the postmodern.* London: Routledge.

Miller, P., & Rose, N. (1993). Governing economic life. In M. Gane & T. Johnston (Eds.), *Foucault's new domains.* London: Routledge.

Moss, P., & Pence, A. (Eds.). (1994). *Valuing quality in early childhood services.* London: Paul Chapman Publishing.

Popkewitz, T. (1998). *Struggling for the soul.* New York: Teachers College Press.

Readings, B. (1996). *The university in ruins.* Cambridge, MA: Harvard University Press.

Rogoff, B., & Chavajay, P. (1995). What's become of research on the cultural basis of cognitive development? *American Psychologist, 50*(10), 859-877.

Toulmin, S. (1990). *Cosmopolis: The hidden agenda of modernity.* Chicago: University of Chicago Press.

Young, R. (1990). *White mythologies: Writing history and the west.* London: Routledge.

The Contribution of Preschool Education to Chilean Education Reform

Blanca Hermosilla M.
Blanca Hermosilla is National Coordinator of Preschool Education, Ministry of Education-Chile.

I come from a southern part of the world, from a country that has appeared in the news recently as we experience painful reminders of 17 years of military dictatorship. In Chile, we are tending our wounds as we try to build up a democratic country without forgetting or burying the past.

My presentation is in three parts. First, I will describe education in Latin America and the Caribbean, preschool education in Latin America, and the main characteristics of Chilean education reform. Second, I will review the policies about coverage and quality of preschool education in Chile since 1990. Finally, I will discuss the results of policies for expansion of services and improvement of quality with equity in Chilean preschools.

EDUCATION IN LATIN AMERICA AND THE CARIBBEAN

A Brief Description of the Region

In 1998, according to the United Nations Population Information Network (1999), the total population of Latin America and the Caribbean was 503.5 million; the population in the Region of the Americas, including Canada and the United States, was 928.1 million. The projected population for the year 2025 is calculated to be 696.7 million for Latin America and the Caribbean, and 1 billion, 196.2 million for the whole region. More than 65 percent of the population in Latin America is concentrated in Brazil (165.9 million), Mexico, (95.8 million), Colombia (40.8 million), and Argentina (36.1 million). There is a native population in the Americas of about 40 million people, composed of 400 ethnic groups; this feature characterizes the Region of the Americas as multiethnic, multicultural, and multilingual.

In Latin America and the Caribbean, 95 million people under 15 years of age live in poverty and 32 million live in extreme poverty. On the threshold of the 21st century, more than 20 million children do not have access to primary school. Forty-seven percent of children who enter primary school do not complete primary education, and millions finish without acquiring essential knowledge and skills. An estimated 2,000 children die every day because of poverty. Poverty is passed from one generation to another, along with health problems, malnutrition, school dropout, early insertion into work, and low productivity.

On average, Latin America and the Caribbean have the highest levels of income per capita in the developing world ($2,000 U.S.). However, that high average hides the fact that income levels in Bolivia, Guyana, and Haiti are as low as in countries of South Africa and the Sahara. Even in the more affluent countries, extreme poverty can be found in rural areas, areas surrounding urban centers, and in certain regions of few natural resources. The distribution of income is critically unequal.

Concerning public expenditure for education and health, the World Bank (1995) reported that the following countries designate the highest percentages of their budgets to education: Costa Rica (19.1 percent), Ecuador (18.2 percent), Belize (16.8 percent), Bolivia (16.6 percent), and Panama (16.1 percent). Countries that commit the lowest percentages to education are the United States (1.8 percent), Canada (2.9 percent), and Brazil (3.7 percent). The biggest budgets for health are in Costa Rica (32 percent, the highest in the world), Panama (21.8 percent), and the United States (16 percent), followed by the Dominican Republic (14 percent) and Chile (11.1 percent).

Education in Latin America

We can confirm that the educational systems of the region have improved access to primary education. Levels of quality appropriate for current demands, however, are in doubt. Although coverage has increased in all levels of education, the most effort has been for children between 5 and 6 years old. This practice does not allow educators to take advantage of the intense neural development that occurs before 2 years of age.

Advances in education are slow, and severe problems affect most of the educational systems of the region, as indicated by low academic performance, repetition of grade, and lack of school completion. Other more qualitative indicators of poor quality in education include deficient educational practices, poor physical conditions of schools, the lack of timely care for children under 6, and the unavailability of books and other resources for pupils and teachers. Pupils' nutritional needs are not being adequately met. Another central problem is the lack of culturally relevant curricula. We also must mention the unsuitable preparation of and remuneration for many teachers. The lack of opportunity and/or flexibility to use more efficient methodologies with students, combined with lack of parental and community participation in the educational process are problems, as well. All these issues must be addressed in order to achieve better quality and equity, and to diminish poverty levels.

The relationship between culture and development is changing toward a wider and progressive concept. As a result, quality programs are diminishing the inequities affecting our populations. However, although we have laws in our region that ensure the right of obligatory primary school, and national averages of access, there are still deep inequities and disparities in quality and quantity of educational opportunities.

Important challenges in the region remain: poverty that affects mainly children, women, and isolated populations; high averages of malnutrition (approximately 41 percent in the region); low level of scholarship and educational quality; and low percentage of care for children between birth and 5 years of age. In addition, intrafamiliar and social violence has increased during the last years, indicating new aspects of mental health that have not been deeply studied.

Preschool Education in Latin America

Within education as a whole, preschool education has experienced the most growth during the last 15 years. The programs are developed in a conventional manner through institutionalized preschool centers, kindergartens, and nurseries administered by the government, or individuals authorized by the government. Indirect services to children are delivered through adult training programs designed to improve parenting or caretaking skills and through psychosocial development programs. Care programs focus on children of higher preschool ages, who are approaching entrance to primary education. Early stimulation and health programs give preference to children under three years of age.

Nonscholarship programs for community development and care for mothers and families have experienced high participation by mothers and parents. These programs, which were initiated as experimental programs 30 years ago (in Columbia, Cuba, Chile, El Salvador, Guatemala, Nicaragua, Peru, and Venezuela), constitute one of Latin America's contributions to global education.

The accelerated expansion of preschool programs represents one of the more important achievements of educational systems in Latin American and the Caribbean over the last decades (Rivero, 1998). In the decade of the 1990s, according to national statistics of Panama, Nicaragua, El Salvador, Bolivia, Venezuela, and Chile, expansion of preschool programs has increased significantly over the last five years. "However, from such progress of the coverage of the preschool child, the situation is far from being satisfactory. It only covers a small group of [the] population: two-thirds of the children 5 years old and a little more than one-fourth of children between 3 and 4 years old" (Rivero, 1998).

Programs for preschool children are different for children with better economic conditions. The private sector plays an important role in providing initial or preschool education to sectors of the population who can pay. One fourth of preschool education in the region is private.

The concept of "quality" tends to be a problem in preschool. Some people fundamentally associate it with physical environment and working materials, while others consider the ratio of children to adults. The number of pupils per teacher in private programs tends to be smaller. Quality also relates to the participation of parents and their own preparation as educational agents (Rivero, 1998).

As a summary:

- Preschool development in Latin America is varied and mainly concentrated on children within one year of entering primary school.
- There are wide variations among the countries in the level of coverage, which are directly related to income level per capita.
- In most of the countries, the percentage of children that attend preschool programs has increased since 1980.
- Care varies in private and public education among countries.
- There is still a deficiency in coverage in urban areas, although explicit efforts have been made to address this in some countries.
- Preschool programs provided to girls and boys are almost identical.
- Preschool programs are less available to lower income groups.
- Preschool programs are less available to native groups.
- Preschool programs are required to implement experiences that facilitate the affective and motor development of boys and girls.

The most important challenge for the future is how to effectively serve groups traditionally isolated from educational opportunities and how to close the gap of educational disparity between the richest and the poorest. Policies and actions concerning preschool children cannot keep on considering boys and girls as objects of care. On the contrary, they must be subjects of rights. Every child, boy or girl, who is not covered in his/her needs of health, education, recreation, security, and protection, is being denied his/her fundamental rights. To protect these rights is the responsibility of the government, of civil society, and of families.

Chilean education reform was born from a policy initiated in March, 1990, with the arrival of democracy. The country is leaving behind 25 years of social and ideological conflict. During this period, education was a relatively isolated area, inevitably harmed by a fight in which the different actors assigned an unequal importance to education. Today, the issue of education overcomes this merely social characterization, and takes its place as a strategic and transverse vector in the group of public policies (Garcia-Huidobro, 1989, 1995; Cox, 1997; Hermosilla, 1998).

At the beginning of the 1990s, Chilean education showed great progress: primary education coverage exceeded 95 percent, and secondary school exceeded 75 percent. Preschool education, however, did not reach 22 percent. To this date, there has been an increase of only 7 percent for preschool education.

The Chilean system is organized around 8 years of obligatory education for children between 6 and 13 years of age, and four nonobligatory years for students between 14 and 17 years of age.

Preschool Education in Chile

Preschool education has a long tradition in Chile. The first preschools, established at the end of the 19th century, were private. Public preschool education was introduced at the beginning the 20th century, as a response to the influence of Maria Montessori and Friedrich Froebel. This kind of education expanded little by little, both in private and public sectors. While preschool education was recognized as part of the formal system of public education in the Primary Obligatory Education Act of 1929, it was made nonobligatory—a feature that remains today.

The career of preschool educator was first formalized at the University of Chile in 1944. The school granted the degree of Preschool Educator to professionals who completed a program of research on children under 6 years, focusing on their growth and development and the proper teaching methods for the learning process. Between 1944 and 1960, preschool education expanded slowly through creation of new kindergartens, foundation of child care centers, and incorporation of programs in public and private schools for girls and boys between 5 and 6 years old. In following years, small children were grouped by age: Nursery Level for children under 2 years, Medium Level for children between 2 and 4 years, and the Transition Level for children between 4 and 6 years of age.

The passage of Law N-17.301 in April 1970 resulted in the establishment of the National Board of Kindergartens, JUNJI, which developed structures and rules for preschool. It also granted fiscal financing for the integral care of children (education, nutrition, and health) from birth until entrance into primary school. The JUNJI began its work in 1971. In 1972, a five-year plan to extend programs in most needed sectors to 40,000 children was implemented.

With the arrival of a military government in 1973, new criteria related to preschool education for children were set. Health and nutrition services for children between birth and 4 years of age were discontinued, and education in kindergartens had to be scientifically guided.

Since 1990, the JUNJI has carried out major institutional renovation, resulting in outstanding advances in the care of children. Programs now have bigger and better educational elements. Currently, the JUNJI takes care of 103,884 children.

Another program, INTEGRA, was first created in 1975 by a former first lady of Chile as FUNACO. In 1990, FUNACO took the name National Foundation for the Integral Development of Children (INTEGRA) and radically changed its objectives and orientation. Currently it serves 57,188 children.

The quality of educational care of small children in Chile is varied, for it depends on different institutions and organizations such as private schools, private-subsidiary schools, municipal schools, the National Board of Kindergartens (JUNJI), and the National Foundation for the Integral Development of Children (INTEGRA). The institutions that take care of children in poverty, especially JUNJI and INTEGRA and municipal schools, have common problems that affect the quality of service, diminishing their capacity to effectively impact children's development and learning. Some of the factors that influenced the quality of care were:

- A shortage of perceptual material for children's work and of support material for family work
- A shortage of personnel at the supervisory level, as well as the classroom level
- Deficiencies in the training of educators that affect pedagogical practices, especially those related to work with low-income adults and those related to language and cognitive development
- Neglect of social communication media as a means to promote and orient an informed and appropriate demand for preschool education services.
- Lack of a national system for evaluation at this level of education that would contribute to planning for and information about cost-effectiveness of different programs.

The consequence of this background was clear: Not all children in Chile had the same educational chances. Therefore, the task was to find new avenues to provide equitable opportunities for all children in Chile.

Policies for Preschool Education Since 1990

Preschool education policies in the 1990s set the goals of improved quality and increased equity, in a context of decentralization and participation. This purpose was designed to be carried out through initiatives directly financed by the government budget and through the Improvement Program for Equity and Quality in Education (MECE).

The MECE program, developed by the Ministry of Education focused on endowment of perceptual materials, incorporation of specialized personnel, and allocation of larger financial resources to expand the number of children served. MECE acted directly, contributing resources to benefit the small children who attended the second transition level of municipal and private-subsidiary institutions. It also benefited children under 6 years who attended nonconventional programs that were the responsibility of the Ministry of Education, by means of agreements with JUNJI and INTEGRA.

In 1994, the preschool component of the MECE Program was institutionalized in the Unit of Preschool Education from the Division of General Education, becoming a specialized level within the school system. This institutionalization formally recognized the importance of this educative level; allowed systemic relationships with other levels, especially with primary school; and incorporated technical and pedagogical features of preschool education.

Improvement of Quality
Initiatives encouraged since 1990 to ensure high-quality and equitable education, mainly for children under 6 from poor areas, include:

- Improvement of the ratio of children to adults.
- Improvement of personnel preparation through programs to train supervisors of preschools in working with adults, popular education, cultural belonging, language development, new approaches to literacy preparation, initiation of science, development of self-respect, project methodology, working as a team, etc.
- Endowment of perceptual material, financed by resources from the MECE Program and benefiting approximately 400,000 children under 6 years who live in poverty conditions.

In 1993, the Ministry of Education transferred financial resources to JUNJI and INTEGRA, permitting those institutions to develop their own procedures for selecting materials. Educators in metropolitan regions were invited to become familiar with available perceptual materials and to determine their preferences based on preschool children's characteristics and the work done in their institution. Some of the materials delivered to schools are mathematics bars, logic blocks, puzzles, construction boxes, dolls of both sexes, transportation toys, musical instruments, dominoes, balls, and traditional games. In general, these materials are accompanied by teaching guides. In 1998, 28,650 children were the beneficiaries of such perceptual materials.

Family Training Programs: The Family As Primary Educator
The Ministry of Education developed the program "Family and Education Centers," in which teams of classroom teachers, parents, and directors joined forces to develop courses to help parents support the development of their children's language skills and logical, mathematical, social, and emotional thinking. This program was funded through a grant from the Educational Television of The Catholic University (TELEDUC) and benefited 4,248 families, whose children attended 1,346 institutions. This program permitted a wider availability of school to the family, a joint search for pedagogical and methodological criteria to improve educational practices, and a forging of connections among educational levels. This experience is a very significant one for Chile; for the first time in 25 years, a link between families and schools is beginning to form.

A second national program implemented in municipal and private-subsidiary schools is called "Manolo and Margarita Learn With Their Parents." This program provides support to preschool educators who work with families. Each mother and father receive a complete set of pictures to be used to facilitate language development, and to improve verbal and affective communications between parents and children in the home. INTEGRA has developed their own programs related to families with topics such as prevention of child maltreatment, resiliency, discrimination, and television habits.

Parental education also has been initiated using mass media. In 1993, the Ministry of Education created an internal institutional committee to launch an educational campaign through TV and the radio that supports parents in their efforts to stimulate their children's development. The messages were designed to help parents recognize that they should express their love for their children through caresses, gestures, attitude, and words. The campaign used modeling as the basic communication technique.

Evaluation of Preschool Programs

The impact of preschool education on children's learning process has been evaluated. Such evaluations meet the need for valid comparative information at the national level that provides feedback on how well efforts to improve quality and equity are succeeding. Between 1994 and 1997, three evaluation studies were conducted. One related to the preschool education programs of widest coverage in the country. Another study measured the impact of the "Get To Know Your Child" program, a nonformal program directed toward children under 6 who live in rural sectors and who do not have access to care programs. The third study evaluated the results of improvements to nonformal programs that are designed and implemented through community participation. The evaluations indicated the following:

- Preschool education programs affect the psychosocial development of children, with greater impact on rural than on urban populations, and more influence in the social and emotional dimension than in the cognitive domain
- Not all experiences are equally effective, at least in the area of cognitive development; children who attend the Second Transition Level in subsidiary schools benefit more than those who attend programs dependent on other institutions
- Preschool education shows a sustained impact on the performance of children from rural sectors; for these children, it is a disadvantage to enter primary school without preschool experience
- Children in the "Get To Know Your Child" program advanced when mothers were committed to participation and demonstrated the value they have for perceptual materials
- In the Improvement Projects for Childhood (PMI), mothers noticed improvements in children's performance, family relationships, and community participation.

Conclusion

The inclusion of the preschool component in the MECE Program and the resulting higher care coverage for small children in Chile helped develop a consciousness about the need to expand preschool education. In this way, political sensibility about this issue has stopped being a central topic and new attention is focused on the tasks of designing pertinent and feasible strategies to increase coverage in sectors with higher social, economical, and cultural vulnerability.

In the 1990s, the Chilean government has launched several efforts to improve the quality of education offered. However, there is much left to do. One pending topic is curricular reform. The challenge will be to incorporate funding, curricular innovations, and the vast experience accumulated by JUNJI, INTEGRA, and the Ministry of Education.

References

Cox, C. (1997). *The reform of Chilean education: Context, contents, implementation.* Santiago, Chile: Ministry of Education.

Garcia-Huidobro, J. E. (1989). *School, quality, and equity, the challenges of educating in democracy.* Santiago, Chile: CIDE.

Garcia-Huidobro, J. E. (1995). *Primary school education: Situation and policies, Dialogue on Education.* Santiago, Chile: Ministry of Education.

Hermosilla, B. (1998). *Preschool education in the reform: A contribution to equity.* Santiago, Chile: Ministry of Education.

Rivero, J. (1998, December). Initial education in the 21st century. *UNESCO Report, 47.*

United Nations Population Information Network. (1999). *World population 1998* [Online]. Available: www.undp.org/popin/wdtrends/p98/098.htm.

World Bank. (1995). *World development indicators.* Washington, DC: Author.

What Kinds of Future for Our Children?

Bettye Caldwell
Bettye Caldwell is Professor of Pediatrics, Child Development and Education at the University of Arkansas for Medical Sciences.

Like birthdays and New Year's Eves, the dawn of a new millennium is a good time to look back at where we have been, and to peer ahead through the mists of uncertainty toward where we are going. It is unlikely that any of us will be present to celebrate the dawn of the 22nd century. If life expectancy figures continue to climb as they have during the 20th century, however, quite a few of the children currently participating in our programs will live to celebrate that event. And they undoubtedly will influence the history that gets written during the next hundred—or thousand—years. Recognition of this reality should intensify our respect for the work we do, as we are privileged to help create the adults who will guide the future. The future that our children claim *can only be what we give them, both internally and externally—internally with respect to capacities and values and predispositions to behavior, and externally with respect to the resources and/or limitations of the physical environment.* That is, the future they can claim will depend on what they become and what they have to work with. Who has major responsibility for both of those contingencies? Educators do. In recognition of this responsibility, please reflect on exactly what kind of future we want to give our children.

FUTURISTIC THINKING ABOUT CHILDREN

When it comes to thinking about the future, we can be crystal clear about some of the things we want to see happen. We want to make sure we do not deplete too many of the natural resources available to us. We know we need to avoid letting the population exceed the limits of sustainability. We know we do not want to deplete the ozone layer, heat up the atmosphere or melt the polar caps. When it comes to articulating what we want *from* our children in the future, however, we fall back on generalities: "We want them to be what they're capable of becoming." "We want them to be happy and productive." Or we might even be focused enough on the reality of our own lives to say, "We want them to be able and willing to take care of us when we need it." We resist getting too specific, or we even refuse to think about it at all. Whether we like to admit it or not, however, the future comes from the present and the past—"our time," if you will.

For many years, I have been a member of the World Future Society. I am fascinated by predictions of future transportation, communication, and environmental protection. About three years ago, a famous futurist published his list of the 10 most important trends in world history. Would you believe that the list did not even mention what might happen in family life, or specifically the world-wide trend for mothers to enter the work force when their children are younger and younger.

My comments on this blatant omission were published as a Letter to the

Editor, but the author of the list did not respond. Families? Children? What have they got to do with the future of life in a technological society? Just everything, that's all. What matters, most futurists would imply, is how fast a message can be transmitted and through what kind of medium. Unfortunately, speed of message transmission has little to do with accuracy of processing once the message reaches the human brain, or with the action likely to be generated by the message.

What I am suggesting here is that in order to help our children we need to *be more specific about the kinds of traits most likely to enable them to claim their future and create a favorable one for their own children.* To do that, we have to be willing to specify exactly what we regard as a livable future, in terms of those aspects for which we have responsibility and that are crucial for allowing our children to claim what is rightfully theirs. While the following five aspects of a desirable future may seem prosaic and obvious, thus far we have not managed to achieve any of them adequately.

CHARACTERISTICS OF A WORTHWHILE FUTURE FOR CHILDREN

Safety and Security

Recently, my husband and I had a thrilling vacation in Egypt. When we were in Luxor, we overheard whispers such as, "Just where was the bus last year when the terrorists blew it up?" Right now, more than a million people in the Balkans are refugees without a home, and at least 100,000 of them are children. In Africa, children are tortured and slaughtered and conscripted into guerilla groups when they are no more than 10 years old. Every day we see pictures in the newspaper of children who have lost a leg by stepping on a land mine. Young children in America write and speak poignantly about their fear of being shot in their homes or randomly on the streets or even on their school playgrounds. In many of our schools, children are afraid to go to the rest room. Two locations that would have meant nothing a few years ago are now stamped indelibly in the minds of most Americans—Jonesboro, Arkansas, and Littleton, Colorado. In these pleasant small cities children sophisticated in the use of guns killed several of their classmates and teachers.

These grisly and depressing reminders of extreme violence are but the tip of the iceberg when it comes to violence against children. Daily we encounter chilling statistics about the magnitude of child abuse in America; Perry (1994) says that at least 5 million children a year in the United States are either victims or observers of violence in their homes or communities. In a more recent paper, he laments, ". . . sadly, in today's world, millions of children are raised in unstable and violent settings. Literally, incubated in terror" (Perry, 1997). Furthermore, there is evidence (Halperin et al., 1995; Lewis, Mallouh, & Webb, 1989; Loeber et al., 1993) that being a witness to violence (e.g., seeing the mother beaten up) produces similar effects in the brain to those associated with being an actual victim.

Physical violence is not the only threat to children's safety. Far more children experience neglect, either physical or emotional. This, of course, is more difficult to document. In the United States, we do not like to admit the prevalence of severe neglect. Yet a coroner's report will describe a 25-pound 6-year-old who has been kept tied up in a closet. These children are there, and they are not all living in poverty.

The concept of "attachment security," which has generated a great deal of empirical research and has become a basic tenet of clinical usage during the past two decades, has direct relevance to the issue of emotional neglect. In a multitude of U.S. studies (see Karen, 1994), it has been found that roughly one-fourth of children do not develop a secure attachment to their mothers and that such children subsequently have more behavioral and learning problems in school and at home.

Some people have questioned whether the experience of being enrolled in child care at an early age might interfere with the development of secure attachment. Some writers (e.g., Belsky, 1986) proclaim this theory flamboyantly in articles and on national television. Others have rebutted it with equal vehemence (e.g., McCartney & Phillips, 1988). With regard to emotional neglect, findings from the large, multi-site Study of Early Child Care (NICHD Early Child Care Research Network, 1997) are of direct relevance. This study indicates that maternal sensitivity, not child care per se, appears to be the more dominant influence on attachment security. In a study of more than 1,000 children, it was found that low maternal sensitivity was associated with absence of secure attachment regardless of whether or for how many hours a week the children were enrolled in child care.

What are the implications of violence and neglect for us as parents and teachers? It seems to me that they are profound. Once children come into our "melting pots," we are expected to facilitate the same kinds and levels of achievement in all of them, regardless of their personal level of security. Somehow, we need to find ways to adapt teaching styles more appropriately to the background conditions that children bring with them. Teaching a securely attached child, one who can readily transfer that attachment to other adults who will assume roles of temporary importance in their lives, is not the same as teaching a child who has never learned to trust anyone.

A second major implication of the high level of violence in the lives of many children relates to our responsibility to help children—regardless of their home backgrounds—learn to find peaceful ways to solve problems, to respect and support one another, and, perhaps most of all, to respect themselves. To me, this indicates that we need to make a major commitment to include what some have called *character education,* but which I prefer to call simply, *"Golden Rule Behavior."* The school must be an environment in which the Golden Rule is lived, not preached.

In a recent article in the *Child Care Information Exchange,* David Elkind (1998), whose work has been very influential in early childhood, asserts boldly that character education is a waste of time. To buttress his claim he cites two studies done in the 1930s and one in the 1970s and completely ignores all the current efforts to develop and evaluate such programs. This assertion bothered me sufficiently that I wrote a rebuttal to it (Caldwell, 1999b). There are at least two methods of fostering character education: curricular infusion and special curriculum units. Both appear to have advantages, and both support our efforts to provide a future for our children that will offer them safety and security. In a recent publication (Caldwell, 1999c), I have described some of the more promising educational efforts to achieve this.

Acceptance of and Respect for Diversity
It is gratifying that OMEP, by definition a diverse organization, and ACEI, a childhood association with concern for global developments in the field, sponsored this Symposium. Headquartered in the United States, ACEI deserves

credit for putting the word "International" into its name and, for more than 30 years, using its meetings and publications to help early education programs become truly multicultural.

I wish to express my hope that future programs we provide for our children will expose them to more than one language during the critical early years when picking up a second language is almost as easy as picking up the first. Some exciting recent research done by Patricia Kuhl and her colleagues has demonstrated that babies younger than 6 months of age can respond to all the sounds that appear in all the world's known languages. If a baby doesn't hear all of those sounds, however, her ability to discriminate among them diminishes rapidly. One implication of this, writes Kuhl (1996, p. 14), is that "they challenge the practice of teaching foreign languages in college [or] even high school. They suggest that languages should be taught in preschool, when children can readily master two languages simultaneously."

Of course, respect for diversity must transcend language. It also must embrace religion and ethnicity—often stirred together in brews of hatred and prejudice. The conflict in Kosovo is a good example of that sort of witches' brew. The bombing in the summer of 1999 of not one but three Jewish temples in Sacramento, California, is another example. We might have come a long way in developing ethnic and religious tolerance, but we still have a long way to go. In helping our children claim their future, we must make absolutely certain that it will be characterized by acceptance of racial, religious, and even economic diversity. Otherwise, we will put up such barriers of hatred and fear that the future will not be worth claiming.

Opportunities for Each Child To Develop Fully

This has been a goal of early childhood care and education from the start. During the 18th and 19th centuries, Comenius, Froebel, and Pestalozzi in Czechoslovakia, Germany, and Switzerland, respectively, strove to teach in ways that respected and encouraged individual talents. In the early years of the 19th century, Robert Owen in Lanarck, Scotland, gave the children of textile workers a chance in life. Maria Montessori worked in the slums of Rome in the latter part of the 19th century. Head Start offered hope for many children in the U.S. starting in the middle of the 20th century. Countless other pioneers have contributed to a tradition that respects *every individual as valuable and deserving of an opportunity to do and be the best and happiest person that that individual is able to become. Furthermore, the tradition asserts, experiences of the first few years of life are critical for allowing that development to occur.* We might say that this is our true early childhood education and care manifesto. This is what we are all about.

The new wave of brain research (see the summary by Shore, 1997) has provided as much of a tonic to the early childhood field as did the mid-20th century launching of a worldwide war on poverty and illiteracy. This new research validates our longheld convictions about the importance of the early years. One often hears the expression that "the brain is not hard-wired at birth," followed by the assertion that, until recently, everyone thought that it was. If indeed some people did think that, early childhood educators were not among them! Such statements coming out of a neuroscience lab seem to have more weight than the same assertion coming from an underpaid and undervalued early childhood professional! We can rejoice that highly regarded basic scientists now are saying things like:

- The first three years of life are a time of amazing growth and change in the brain.
- During this period, it is essential that the child participate in the kinds of experiences that will maximize brain growth and increase efficiency of function.
- There are periods of time—sensitive periods—during development when the brain is especially ready to receive and learn certain kinds of information.
- New learning occurs as synapses (connections) are formed between and among neurons. This development occurs rapidly in the early years, plateaus around 6-8 years, and actually diminishes during subsequent development.
- Living under conditions of deprivation and stress during these critical early years produces chemical changes in the brain that inhibit new learning.

In trying to help young children develop optimally, therefore, we are acting in concert with the latest neuroscience. We need to remember, however, that the word "development" covers a comprehensive array of life events. This means that the services we offer must be comprehensive. While we now typically speak of "education and care" as being our mission (a service for which I have urged adoption of the term *educare*, see Caldwell, 1991), we must not overlook the importance of physical growth and health, social skills, emotional security, and a commitment to be of service to others and the environment.

Valuing Children

It is a vital part of our collective self-concept in America that we deeply value children. I suspect that this is true of all the countries represented at the Symposium. In the States, we always manage to get them in on the top line, but we leave them off the bottom line—the money line, if you will. Recently, I heard Edwin Meese, former U.S. Attorney General, claim that all the publicity about crime in America was exaggerated and that, since 1990, there had been a significant reduction of crime. When pressed for his opinion regarding the reason for the reduction, the speaker asserted that crime had gone down because we have more criminals in prison! Hardly a solution to the problem. And hardly prevention!

In U.S. dollars, it costs around $100,000 per person per year to keep someone in prison. Does anyone know of a school district that spends that much per year on a child? Or of an early childhood teacher who makes that much money in a year? Perhaps that is not a fair comparison, as presumably the amount it costs to keep a person in prison for a year benefits the whole community and does not represent payment to just one person. Yet, does not an adequately loved and educated child benefit the entire society? The disparity between our rhetoric about loving children and the reality of our behavior has been nowhere more powerfully described and documented than by Marian Wright Edelman and her organization, the Children's Defense Fund (CDF). Year after year, they put out depressing statistics about how many children remain unserved in basic health care, about the lack of quality in many child care settings, and about how poverty itself (over and above its associated characteristics like under-education, dysfunctional family life, and unemployment) has negative consequences for children. In spite of a vibrant economy, the number of children in the U.S. (approximately one-fourth of all children) being raised in poverty does not seem to go down (CDF, 1999). UNICEF has attempted to present similar data for children from both developed and developing nations (Bellamy, 1997). In all cases, children tend to appear at the bottom of any list of priorities judged in terms of appropriations.

In the large NICHD Study of Early Child Care (1997), on which I was one of the researchers, we found limited association between child care experiences and child development. Some found this disappointing. In this study, contrary to customary research strategy, family characteristics were assessed right along with child care. In every major data analysis done so far, family characteristics (education, income, presence of father in the home, maternal depression, etc.) have shown more robust associations with child outcomes than age of entry into care or hours per week in care (NICHD Early Child Care Research Network, 1998). Indeed, when we *have* been able to establish an association with child care, it consistently has been the *quality of care* that has shown a relationship to child outcome measures. Certainly, our study is not the first one to demonstrate such an association. Research done in many parts of the U.S., however, shows that care in roughly one-fourth of the studied facilities are of poor quality, with only a small percent classified as of high quality. As child care is a labor-intensive service, quality is highly correlated with cost. Again, the children simply do not get onto the bottom line. To summarize this point, in order for our children to claim a good future, we have to help shape our society into one that truly values children—and allocates funds accordingly.

Firm Governmental Support
All of us, in our native or adopted countries, can point to public policies that support the achievement of *some* of these characteristics of desirable futures. But who among us can boast: "I come from a country where *all* of these goals are recognized and supported by firm legislative mandates, by corporate endorsement, and by public attitudes?" Probably none of us. Most of us live in countries where the service pattern looks like a patchwork quilt—a motheaten one that was made from leftover scraps.

It is my hope that this Symposium will have helped forge a commitment to the development of a comprehensive system of early childhood services. It is clear that we need such a comprehensive system—one that will ensure the availability of a full spectrum of services ranging along several axes:

- Timing (point of entry from prenatal to elementary school)
- Quantity of Contact (home visiting and parent education to full-day educare)
- Auspice (public or private)
- Nature (preventive or therapeutic)
- Funding Source (parents, business, government at different levels)
- Population Served (socially and economically at risk, potentially or actually disabled, abused, middle class, gifted).

And all of these programs should be of high quality.

When we achieve this, the futures of our children in the new millennium will be unquestionably brighter and happier.

Summary
The Symposium provided an opportunity to explore ways to help create a viable and satisfying future for our children. I have attempted to create a philosophical

framework that outlines the kind of future that we want children to be able to claim. Specifically, I have suggested that we want for them a future that is safe and secure, one that accepts and respects the diversity they represent, one that allows each of them to develop fully, one in which children are deeply and truly valued, and one in which governmental policies are put in place to help achieve the other qualities.

Each April, Americans celebrate Earth Day—a day devoted to paying respect to the earth on which we must all live and which we must protect in order to have any kind of future. Last year for Earth Day I wrote a little poem, which I called A *Prayer for Earth Day* (Caldwell, 1999a). In a way, it encapsulates everything I have tried to say in this paper.

A Prayer for Earth Day

Mother Earth . . .

With all your bounty you have nourished us,
have freely fed and watered, cooled and warmed.
Accepting all your gifts quite casually,
we squandered wantonly, now search, alarmed,

for ways to offer recompense to you.
To cancel out our debt we make this oath:
We pledge our help to raise the kind of child
you need to guarantee your future growth.

To do this we ourselves must grow and change,
for in the past we acted otherwise,
and somehow let resources slip away,
defeating our intents with compromise.

No more.

The time has come for new resolve to spring.
When children get their due, the earth will sing.

References

Bellamy, C. (1997). *The state of the world's children, 1997.* New York: Oxford University Press.

Belsky, J. (1986). Infant day care: A cause for concern? *Zero to Three, 6,* 1-6.

Caldwell, B. M. (1991). Educare: New product, new future. *Journal of Developmental and Behavioral Pediatrics, 12,* 199-205.

Caldwell, B. M. (1999a). A prayer for Earth Day. *Young Children, 54,* 52.

Caldwell, B. M. (1999b). Character education: A curricular necessity. *Child Care Information Exchange, May,* 40, 42, 44.

Caldwell, B. M. (1999c). The role of education in the prevention of violence. In J. Gomes-Pedro (Ed.), *Stress and violence in childhood and youth* (pp. 555-576). Lisbon, Portugal: Faculty of Medicine, University of Lisbon.

Children's Defense Fund. (1999). *The state of America's children yearbook.* Washington, DC: Children's Defense Fund.

Elkind, D. (1998). Character education: An ineffective luxury? *Child Care Information*

Exchange, November, 6-9.

Halperin, J. M., Newcorn, J. H., Matier, K., Bedi, G., Hall, S., & Sharma, V. (1995). Impulsivity and the initiation of fights in children with disruptive behavioral disorders. *Journal of Child Psychology and Psychiatry, 36,* 1199-1211.

Karen, R. (1994). *Becoming attached.* San Francisco: Jossey-Bass.

Kuhl, P. K. (1996). How babies map their native languages. In *Bridging the gap between neuroscience and education* (pp. 13-14). Denver, CO: Education Commission of the States.

Lewis, D. O., Mallouh, C., & Webb, V. (1989). Child abuse, delinquency, and violent criminality. In D. Chiccetti & V. Carlson (Eds.), *Child maltreatment: Theory and research on the causes and consequences of child abuse and neglect.* Cambridge: Cambridge University Press.

Loeber, R., Wung, P., Keenan, K., Giroux, B., Stouthamer-Loeber, M., Van Kammen, W. B., & Maughan, B. (1993). Developmental pathways in disruptive child behavior. *Developmentand Psychopathology, 5,* 103-133.

McCartney, K., & Phillips, D. (1988). Motherhood and child care. In B. Birns & D. Hay (Eds.), *The different faces of motherhood* (pp. 157-183). New York: Plenum.

NICHD Early Child Care Research Network. (1997). The effects of infant child care on infant-mother attachment security: Results of the NICHD Study of Early Child Care. *Child Development, 68,* 860-879.

NICHD Early Child Care Research Network. (1998). Early child care and self-control, compliance, and problem behavior at twenty-four and thirty-six months. *Child Development, 69,* 1145-1170.

Perry, B. D. (1994). Neurobiological sequelae of childhood trauma: Posttraumatic stress disorders in children. In M. Murberg (Ed.), *Catecholamines in posttraumatic stress disorder: Emerging concepts* (pp. 253-276). Washington, DC: American Psychiatric Association Press.

Perry, B. D. (1997). Incubated in terror: Neurodevelopmental factors in the "Cycle of Violence." In J. D. Osofsky (Ed.), *Children in a violent society* (pp. 124-149). New York: Guilford Publications.

Shore, R. (1997). *Rethinking the brain.* New York: Families and Work Institute.

Association for Childhood
Education International
17904 Georgia Avenue, Suite 215
Olney, Maryland 20832
1-800-423-3563 • www.acei.org

World Organization for
Early Childhood Education
(Organisation Mondiale pour
l'Éducation Préscolaire)